I WONDER WHY THE STARS TWINKLE?

PUBLISHED IN MOONSTONE
BY RUPA PUBLICATIONS INDIA PVT. LTD 2026
161-B/4, GULMOHAR HOUSE,
YUSUF SARAI COMMUNITY CENTRE,
NEW DELHI 110049

SALES CENTRES:
BENGALURU CHENNAI
HYDERABAD KOLKATA MUMBAI

P-ISBN: 978-93-7003-278-1
E-ISBN: 978-93-7003-711-3
FIRST IMPRESSION 2026

10 9 8 7 6 5 4 3 2 1

PRINTED IN INDIA

Table Of Contents

Why Do Stars Twinkle?

Do stars really flicker?

YES, BUT THE TWINKLE ISN'T FROM THE STARS THEMSELVES. THEIR LIGHT PASSES THROUGH EARTH'S RESTLESS ATMOSPHERE, WHICH BENDS AND SHAKES THE BEAMS, MAKING THEM LOOK LIKE THEY ARE SPARKLING.

How does the air do that?

AIR ABOVE US IS NEVER STILL. SHIFTING LAYERS OF WARM AND COOL AIR BEND STARLIGHT IN MANY DIRECTIONS, CAUSING TINY CHANGES THAT OUR EYES SEE AS TWINKLING PATTERNS.

Do all stars twinkle ?

FROM EARTH THEY DO, BECAUSE OF OUR ATMOSPHERE. BUT IN SPACE, WHERE THERE'S NO AIR TO BEND THE LIGHT, STARS SHINE CLEARLY AND STEADILY, WITHOUT A SINGLE FLICKER.

Why don't planets twinkle ?

PLANETS LOOK BIGGER IN OUR SKY, SO THEIR LIGHT SPREADS THROUGH THE ATMOSPHERE MORE EVENLY. THIS MAKES THEIR GLOW STEADIER, UNLIKE STARS WHICH APPEAR AS SHARP SINGLE POINTS.

What Are Stars Made Of?

Are stars solid balls?

NO, STARS ARE HUGE, GLOWING SPHERES OF GAS. THEY ARE MOSTLY HYDROGEN AND HELIUM, BURNING BRIGHTLY THROUGH NUCLEAR REACTIONS THAT RELEASE ENOUGH LIGHT TO BE SEEN ACROSS SPACE.

What makes them shine?

IN A STAR'S CORE, HYDROGEN ATOMS FUSE TOGETHER UNDER EXTREME HEAT AND PRESSURE. THIS PROCESS, CALLED NUCLEAR FUSION, CREATES HELIUM AND RELEASES POWERFUL BURSTS OF LIGHT AND ENERGY.

Is our sun a star too?

YES, THE SUN IS OUR NEAREST STAR. BECAUSE IT'S SO CLOSE, IT LOOKS ENORMOUS COMPARED WITH OTHERS. BUT IT'S JUST ONE AMONG BILLIONS IN THE MILKY WAY.

Are all stars the same size?

NO. STARS COME IN MANY SIZES. SOME ARE SMALL RED DWARFS, BURNING FAINTLY. OTHERS ARE GIANT SUPERSTARS, HUNDREDS OF TIMES BIGGER THAN THE SUN, BLAZING FIERCELY AND BRILLIANTLY.

How Far Away Are Stars?

Are stars close to us?

NO, MOST STARS ARE UNIMAGINABLY FAR AWAY. THE NEAREST STAR AFTER THE SUN, PROXIMA CENTAURI, IS MORE THAN 40 TRILLION KILOMETRES FROM EARTH, FAR BEYOND OUR REACH.

If they're so far, why can we see them?

BECAUSE STARS ARE HUGE AND POWERFUL, SHINING WITH INCREDIBLE BRIGHTNESS. THEIR LIGHT TRAVELS ACROSS EMPTY SPACE UNTIL IT REACHES US, FAINT BUT STILL VISIBLE AGAINST THE DARK SKY.

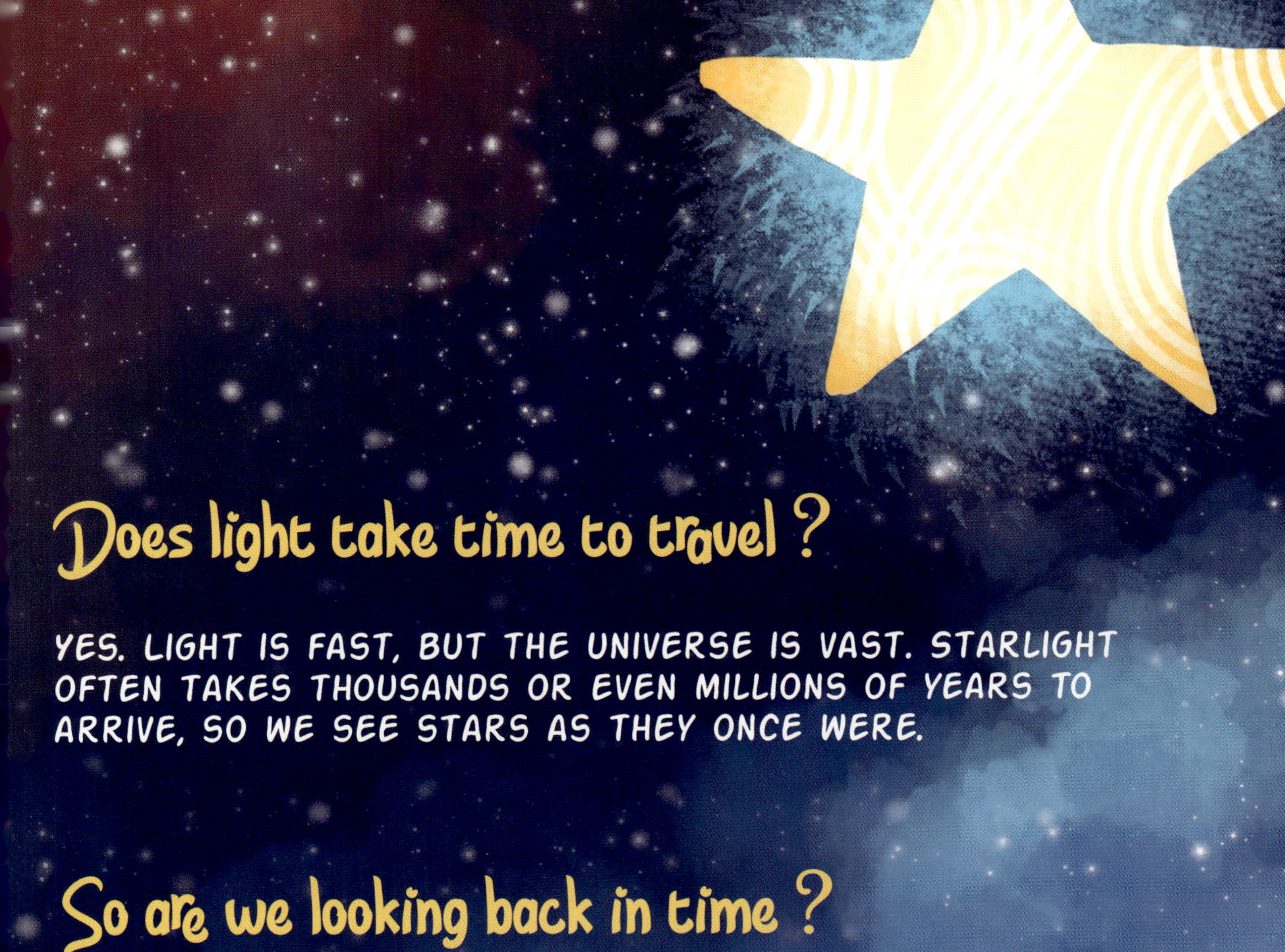

Does light take time to travel?

YES. LIGHT IS FAST, BUT THE UNIVERSE IS VAST. STARLIGHT OFTEN TAKES THOUSANDS OR EVEN MILLIONS OF YEARS TO ARRIVE, SO WE SEE STARS AS THEY ONCE WERE.

So are we looking back in time?

EXACTLY! EVERY STAR IN THE NIGHT SKY SHOWS US THE PAST. SOME MAY HAVE ALREADY CHANGED OR DIED, BUT THEIR ANCIENT LIGHT IS ONLY NOW REACHING EARTH.

Why Do Stars Look Different?

Are all stars white?

NO. STARS COME IN MANY COLOURS: RED, ORANGE, YELLOW, BLUE, OR WHITE. THEIR COLOUR DEPENDS ON TEMPERATURE—COOLER STARS GLOW RED, WHILE HOTTER ONES BLAZE BRIGHT BLUE OR WHITE.

Which stars are hottest?

BLUE STARS ARE THE HOTTEST, WITH TEMPERATURES OF TENS OF THOUSANDS OF DEGREES. RED STARS ARE COOLER, THOUGH STILL FAR HOTTER THAN ANYTHING ON EARTH'S SURFACE.

Why are some stars brighter than others?

SOME STARS LOOK BRIGHT BECAUSE THEY ARE NEARBY, OTHERS BECAUSE THEY ARE MASSIVE AND POWERFUL. DISTANCE, SIZE, AND HEAT TOGETHER DECIDE HOW BRIGHT A STAR APPEARS IN OUR SKY.

Can stars change colour?

YES. AS STARS AGE, THEIR COLOURS SHIFT. HOT BLUE STARS CAN SWELL INTO COOLER RED GIANTS, BEFORE SHRINKING INTO WHITE DWARFS THAT GLOW FAINTLY IN THEIR FINAL YEARS.

How Many Stars Are There?

Can we count them all?

NO, THERE ARE FAR TOO MANY. ASTRONOMERS ESTIMATE HUNDREDS OF BILLIONS OF STARS IN OUR GALAXY ALONE, AND COUNTLESS MORE SPREAD ACROSS BILLIONS OF DISTANT GALAXIES.

What is a galaxy?

A GALAXY IS A MASSIVE COLLECTION OF STARS, GAS, AND DUST, BOUND TOGETHER BY GRAVITY. GALAXIES CAN BE SPIRAL, OVAL, OR IRREGULAR, FLOATING LIKE ISLANDS IN SPACE.

What's our galaxy called?

WE LIVE IN THE MILKY WAY, A SPIRAL-SHAPED GALAXY. ON A CLEAR NIGHT, WE SEE IT AS A SILVERY BAND OF LIGHT STRETCHING ACROSS THE SKY.

Are there more galaxies?

YES, POSSIBLY TRILLIONS. EACH ONE HOLDS BILLIONS OF STARS. ALTOGETHER, THE UNIVERSE CONTAINS MORE STARS THAN THERE ARE GRAINS OF SAND ON EVERY BEACH ON EARTH.

Why Do Some Stars Form Patterns?

What are constellations?

CONSTELLATIONS ARE GROUPS OF STARS JOINED INTO PATTERNS BY OUR IMAGINATION. THEY LOOK LIKE ANIMALS, PEOPLE, OR OBJECTS, HELPING US RECOGNISE AND REMEMBER DIFFERENT PARTS OF THE SKY.

Who made up the patterns?

ANCIENT CULTURES INVENTED THEM. FARMERS USED THEM TO TRACK SEASONS, TRAVELLERS USED THEM TO GUIDE JOURNEYS, AND STORYTELLERS FILLED THE SKY WITH MYTHS ABOUT HEROES AND MAGICAL CREATURES.

Do constellations move ?

THEY SEEM TO MOVE AS EARTH SPINS, RISING AND SETTING LIKE THE SUN. BUT THE STARS THEMSELVES ARE FIXED IN SPACE, ONLY SHIFTING VERY SLOWLY OVER THOUSANDS OF YEARS.

Can everyone see the same ones ?

NO. PEOPLE IN THE NORTHERN HEMISPHERE SEE CONSTELLATIONS LIKE THE BIG DIPPER. IN THE SOUTH, STARGAZERS INSTEAD SEE CONSTELLATIONS SUCH AS THE SOUTHERN CROSS SPARKLING OVERHEAD.

Why Do Stars Help Us Navigate?

How did sailors use stars?

BEFORE MAPS OR SATELLITES, SAILORS READ THE NIGHT SKY. THEY USED CONSTELLATIONS TO FOLLOW THEIR ROUTES, KNOWING FAMILIAR PATTERNS ALWAYS ROSE AND SET IN PREDICTABLE PLACES.

Which star shows the way north?

THE NORTH STAR, OR POLARIS, HARDLY MOVES IN THE SKY. IT ALWAYS POINTS NORTH, GUIDING TRAVELLERS AND SAILORS FOR CENTURIES, ESPECIALLY IN THE NORTHERN HALF OF EARTH.

Can stars tell the time ?

YES. PEOPLE ONCE USED THE RISING AND SETTING OF CERTAIN STARS TO MEASURE HOURS, MARK SEASONS, AND PLAN FARMING OR FESTIVALS LONG BEFORE MODERN CLOCKS WERE INVENTED.

Do we still use stars to travel ?

TODAY SATELLITES GUIDE US MORE ACCURATELY. BUT STARS REMAIN A RELIABLE BACKUP, AND THEY ARE STILL USED BY ADVENTURERS, SAILORS, AND EVEN MIGRATING ANIMALS TO NAVIGATE.

Do Stars Live Forever ?

Are stars born ?

YES. STARS ARE BORN IN ENORMOUS CLOUDS OF DUST AND GAS CALLED NEBULAE. GRAVITY PULLS THE MATERIAL TOGETHER UNTIL IT BEGINS TO GLOW AND IGNITE AS A NEW STAR.

Do they grow old ?

YES. STARS SPEND MILLIONS OR BILLIONS OF YEARS BURNING THEIR FUEL. THEIR SIZE DECIDES THEIR LIFE: SMALL STARS LIVE LONGER, WHILE LARGE STARS BURN BRIGHTLY BUT BRIEFLY.

What happens when they die ?

SMALL STARS FADE SLOWLY INTO WHITE DWARFS. BIG STARS EXPLODE IN SPECTACULAR SUPERNOVAS, SENDING GAS AND DUST RUSHING INTO SPACE TO FORM NEW STARS AND PLANETS.

Can new stars be born again ?

YES. THE DUST AND GAS LEFT BEHIND CAN GATHER TOGETHER, COLLAPSE, AND CREATE NEW STARS. IN THIS WAY, THE UNIVERSE IS ALWAYS RECYCLING ITS MATERIALS INTO NEW LIFE.

What Is a Shooting Star?

Is it really a star?

NO, A SHOOTING STAR IS NOT A STAR AT ALL. IT'S A TINY BIT OF ROCK OR DUST FROM SPACE BURNING BRIGHTLY AS IT ENTERS EARTH'S ATMOSPHERE.

Why does it glow?

AS THE ROCK SPEEDS THROUGH THE AIR, IT GETS SO HOT THAT IT BLAZES LIKE FIRE, LEAVING A GLOWING TRAIL OF LIGHT STREAKING QUICKLY ACROSS THE NIGHT SKY.

Can you see lots at once?

YES. DURING METEOR SHOWERS, EARTH PASSES THROUGH CLOUDS OF SPACE DUST, AND DOZENS—OR EVEN HUNDREDS—OF SHOOTING STARS CAN BE SPOTTED EVERY HOUR.

Can one reach Earth?

SOMETIMES. IF A PIECE OF ROCK IS LARGE ENOUGH TO SURVIVE ITS FIERY JOURNEY THROUGH THE ATMOSPHERE, IT LANDS ON EARTH AND IS CALLED A METEORITE.

Why Do Some Stars Explode?

What is a supernova?

A SUPERNOVA IS A MASSIVE EXPLOSION THAT HAPPENS WHEN A HUGE STAR RUNS OUT OF FUEL. IT COLLAPSES INWARDS, THEN BLASTS OUTWARDS WITH UNIMAGINABLE FORCE AND LIGHT.

How bright is it?

FOR A SHORT TIME, ONE SUPERNOVA CAN OUTSHINE AN ENTIRE GALAXY. IT CAN BE MILLIONS OF TIMES BRIGHTER THAN THE SUN, LIGHTING THE SKY EVEN IN DAYLIGHT.

What happens after ?

THE STAR'S CORE MAY TURN INTO A TINY, DENSE NEUTRON STAR. IF THE STAR WAS EXTREMELY MASSIVE, ITS COLLAPSE CAN CREATE A BLACK HOLE WITH POWERFUL GRAVITY.

Are we safe from them ?

YES. THE SUPERNOVAS NEAR US ARE TOO FAR AWAY TO CAUSE HARM. SCIENTISTS STUDY THEIR LIGHT SAFELY THROUGH TELESCOPES, LEARNING ABOUT HOW STARS LIVE AND DIE.

What Is a Black Hole ?

Is it a hole in space ?

NOT EXACTLY. A BLACK HOLE IS A PLACE WHERE GRAVITY IS SO STRONG THAT NOTHING, NOT EVEN LIGHT, CAN ESCAPE. IT FORMS AN INVISIBLE TRAP IN SPACE.

How do they form ?

WHEN VERY MASSIVE STARS COLLAPSE AT THE END OF THEIR LIVES, THEIR CORES SHRINK UNDER INTENSE GRAVITY. THE COLLAPSE SQUEEZES EVERYTHING INTO AN INCREDIBLY TINY, DENSE POINT.

Can we see them ?

NOT DIRECTLY. BLACK HOLES DON'T SHINE. BUT SCIENTISTS DETECT THEM BY WATCHING HOW NEARBY STARS AND GAS SWIRL, VANISH, OR GLOW AS THEY ARE PULLED INWARD.

Would one swallow Earth ?

NO. THE BLACK HOLES CLOSE TO US ARE SAFELY DISTANT. NONE IS NEAR ENOUGH TO THREATEN EARTH, SO WE CAN STUDY THEM WITHOUT FEAR OF BEING SWALLOWED.

Do Stars Make Us ?

What are we made of ?

OUR BODIES CONTAIN CARBON, OXYGEN, IRON, AND OTHER ELEMENTS. THESE ESSENTIAL BUILDING BLOCKS WERE CREATED LONG AGO INSIDE STARS AND SPREAD THROUGH THE UNIVERSE WHEN THOSE STARS EXPLODED.

How did they get here ?

WHEN STARS EXPLODED, THEIR MATERIAL DRIFTED ACROSS SPACE, EVENTUALLY BECOMING PART OF NEW PLANETS, PLANTS, AND PEOPLE. IN THIS WAY, THE MATTER INSIDE US ONCE CAME FROM STARS.

Does that mean we're star-dust ?

YES! EVERY PERSON, PLANT, AND ANIMAL IS BUILT FROM ATOMS FIRST FORMED IN STARS. WE ARE LIVING PROOF THAT THE UNIVERSE RECYCLES ITSELF INTO NEW FORMS OF LIFE.

Are new stars still making elements ?

YES. STARS ACROSS THE UNIVERSE CONTINUE FORGING ELEMENTS, FILLING SPACE WITH THE INGREDIENTS FOR FUTURE PLANETS, CREATURES, AND POSSIBLY EVEN NEW LIFE SOMEWHERE BEYOND OUR OWN WORLD.

Can Stars Be Different Shapes ?

Are stars spiky like they look in drawings ?

NO, REAL STARS ARE ROUND SPHERES OF GAS. THE SPIKY SHAPES IN PICTURES OR PHOTOS ARE TRICKS CAUSED BY OUR EYES OR TELESCOPES BENDING THE LIGHT.

So why do they look spiky ?

WHEN STARLIGHT PASSES THROUGH OUR EYES OR CAMERA LENSES, THE EDGES SCATTER INTO RAYS. THIS MAKES STARS APPEAR TO HAVE SHINING SPIKES, EVEN THOUGH THEY ARE ACTUALLY SMOOTH.

Can stars spin ?

YES. MANY STARS ROTATE, SOME VERY QUICKLY. CERTAIN STARS SPIN SO FAST THEY COMPLETE A TURN IN JUST HOURS, COMPARED WITH EARTH'S 24-HOUR ROTATION.

Can stars have partners ?

YES. MANY STARS LIVE IN PAIRS OR GROUPS, CIRCLING EACH OTHER IN CLUSTERS. THESE SYSTEMS ARE COMMON IN SPACE, WHERE STARS OFTEN FORM TOGETHER IN FAMILIES.

Will Stars Twinkle Forever?

Will stars always be in the sky?

YES, BUT INDIVIDUAL STARS CHANGE. SOME FADE AWAY, OTHERS EXPLODE, AND NEW ONES ARE BORN. THE SKY IS ALWAYS EVOLVING, THOUGH IT LOOKS STEADY FROM NIGHT TO NIGHT.

Could stars crash together?

YES. WHEN GALAXIES COLLIDE, SOME STARS CAN MERGE. THOUGH RARE, THESE POWERFUL EVENTS CREATE BURSTS OF LIGHT AND MAY EVEN FORM NEW, LARGER STARS SHINING EVEN BRIGHTER.

Will new stars replace old ones?

YES. NEBULAE RECYCLE OLD MATERIAL INTO FRESH STARS. THE CYCLE OF BIRTH AND DEATH MEANS THE UNIVERSE WILL NEVER TRULY RUN OUT OF STARS TO LIGHT THE DARKNESS.

So will the night sky always sparkle?

YES! FOR COUNTLESS GENERATIONS TO COME, THE UNIVERSE WILL KEEP SHINING. STARS MAY CHANGE, BUT THEIR TWINKLING BEAUTY WILL ALWAYS BE PART OF OUR NIGHT SKIES.

A mini quiz :

Why do stars twinkle in our night sky?

___

What is the name of our galaxy?

___

What is a shooting star really made of?

___

How are we connected to the stars ourselves?

___